Classic
PAPER
PLANES

hinkler

hinkler

Published by Hinkler Books Pty Ltd
45–55 Fairchild Street
Heatherton Victoria 3202 Australia
www.hinkler.com.au

Cover Design: Hinkler Studio
Design: Sam Grimmer
Photography: Ned Meldrum
Prepress: Graphic Print Group
Typesetting: MPS Limited

ISBN: 978 1 7418 4812 0

Printed and bound in China

Introduction

Paper planes

Paper airplanes are a one-way ticket back to your childhood! Paper planes are the perfect hobby or interest for people of all ages, backgrounds, and level of expertise. Plane making is both stimulating and relaxing. It costs virtually nothing, needs no equipment, and is a low-tech way to have a lot of fun. You can choose to make designs as easy or as relatively difficult as you wish; either way gives a real sense of achievement. Create your planes on your own, as a family, or as a small group and see how fast, high, and long they can fly. Above all, have fun with them!

In *Fold & Fly Paper Planes* there are plenty of designs for you to try. I give step-by-step instructions for 20 planes, many of which are original designs that you won't find anywhere else! Once you have mastered the steps, you are only a piece of paper away from launching your newest creation.

The designs become more complicated as you go through the book, often building on earlier ideas, so if you start at the beginning you should find it easier to tackle the more complex constructions. Alternatively, you can dive right in and start making the planes that most appeal to you. Perhaps you will even be inspired to create some designs of your own!

A brief history of paper airplanes

The first real airplane was designed, built, and flown in 1903 by the Wright brothers. As far as I can tell, the earliest documented paper airplane followed ten years later, in 1913. I am still searching for earlier paper airplane designs; I have read about some from as early as 700 AD!

Some of the first pilots, the "Early Birds," created some very nice paper airplane designs. A standout is Percy Pierce. His patented designs appeared in issues of American women's fashion magazines *McCall's* and *The Delineator* in the 1920s. The planes were quite striking, and fairly complex to assemble.

During the 1940s, great advances occurred in aviation. Planes flew faster and higher, and were more reliable than ever. In this decade the jet engine was born, and all metal planes reigned supreme. As a consequence, the increased knowledge of avionics also improved paper planes. Paper planes became so popular that designs were even featured on cereal boxes. A key designer of the day was Wallis Rigby, who is credited with creating the "tab and slot" method. His planes appeared in newspapers, thrilling readers with their realistic detail. Even today they are a lot of fun to make and fly.

The Great International Paper Airplane Book, published in 1967, introduced the concept of laminate paper airplanes, which were popularized by Dr Yasuaki Ninomiya of Japan in his famous and fantastic *Whitewings* series. Capable of greater speeds, heights, and variety of shapes, some of the models were even propelled by a rubber band launcher, which could catapult them high enough to ride thermals!

A further significant development occurred in the 1970s when Americans Richard Kline and Floyd Fogleman came up with a new airfoil design using paper airplanes as a test bed. Their unique wing shape could also change its thickness, and they eventually patented the concept, which was a real feat! Their 1985 book, *The Ultimate Paper Airplane*, provides plans for seven different models of this groundbreaking design.

Paper airplane competitions

The first international paper airplane competition was held in 1967, sponsored and conducted by *Scientific American*. The competition brought together various styles and forms of paper airplane making from all over the world, which were subsequently published in *The Great*

3

International Paper Airplane Book. The book became a bestseller and many of its designs are among those that are most recognized today.

In 1985 the second international paper airplane contest was held. Conducted by the editors of *Science 86* magazine, it demonstrated how many advances had been made since the first contest eighteen years previously.

The World Record

Takuo Toda, Chairman of the Japan Origami Airplane Association, is the current title holder of the Guinness World Record for time aloft of a paper airplane. He set the record in April 2009, with a time of 27.9 seconds. Prior to Mr Toda breaking the World Record, Ken Blackburn, an aeronautical engineer living in Laurel Hill, Florida, flew a paper plane inside the U.S.A.'s Georgia Dome in 1998 and held the record of 27.6 seconds for over ten years!

A note on paper

The designs in this book were created with and for 20lb (75gsm) A4 paper. While A4 is a very popular size, it is by no means the only one you can use. A size close to A4 is Letter, which is a little shorter and wider than A4. You can still create the designs in this book with Letter size, just keep in mind that the angles on some of the illustrations may not match up, and that the finished plane may need additional tweaking and trimming to fly correctly. You can have plenty of fun experimenting with different types of paper – variations in size, thickness, and rigidity will all produce different results. Don't forget to make your plane look good too! Use colored paper, stickers, patterned paper, or draw your favorite designs onto your plane to make it stand out.

You will see that some planes are constructed from square sheets of paper. To make your own square sheets, fold the top left corner of the A4 paper over to the right side, keeping the top edge of the paper even with the right side. Give it a good crease so the paper will stay in place, then cut off the excess paper on the bottom. Unfold, and you've got your square.

About the author

Growing up in Iowa, Dean Mackey always enjoyed flying paper airplanes. Some of his earliest memories are of flying paper airplanes off the porch and watching them soar over the cliff across the street. His older siblings taught him a few designs, and he learned a few more from the venerable *Great International Paper Airplane Book.*

Dean's skills lay dormant until the year 2000, when he volunteered to work at "Space Day" in Tewksbury, Massachusetts. Researching new designs, Dean was amazed at what he found on the internet. As well as experimenting with his own designs, he started collecting web links that talented people had put online for all to enjoy. A few years later, he launched The Online Paper Airplane Museum, featuring over 800 free paper airplane designs, personal reviews of paper airplane books, and many other items related to paper planes.

Visit The Online Paper Airplane Museum at http://www.theonlinepaperairplanemuseum.com. Questions or comments can be sent to Dean at deanmackey@gmail.com.

This book is dedicated to
Katie (Schmoopie) Mackey.

Aviation Glossary

AILERON
A movable panel at the rear edge of each airplane wing; the aileron can be raised or lowered and cause the plane to bank left or right.

AIRFOIL
The shape of the wing as seen from the side; it is the shape of the wing that causes a plane to lift.

CANARD
A small wing that sits forward of the main wings on the fuselage of a plane.

DIHEDRAL
The position of the wings on a plane relative to the fuselage. If the wings are raised relative to the fuselage, the dihedral is positive. If the wings are lowered, the dihedral is negative.

No dihedral   Positive dihedral   Negative dihedral

ELEVATOR
The control flaps at the rear of an aircraft; the elevator can be raised or lowered and cause the plane to ascend or descend.

FUSELAGE
The main body of a plane; the wings and tail attach to the fuselage of the plane.

Aviation Glossary

RUDDER

A vertical airfoil at the tail of a plane used for steering; the rudder can be moved left or right and cause the plane to move right or left.

SPOILER

A small airfoil, usually found on the rear of a racing car. On the planes in this book, a spoiler is intended to increase lift.

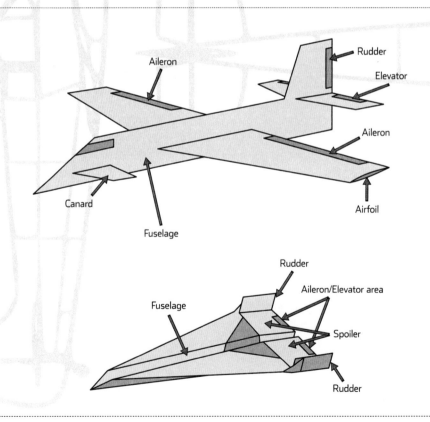

Aileron

Rudder

Elevator

Aileron

Canard

Airfoil

Fuselage

Rudder

Aileron/Elevator area

Fuselage

Spoiler

Rudder

Folding Glossary

FLIP FOLD Fold up along the result of a previous fold.

INSIDE REVERSE FOLD The corner of an existing fold is creased, pushed in, and folded on the inside.

MOUNTAIN FOLD Fold sides together so paper forms a ∧ shape.

PRESS Use your fingers to push the paper in the correct direction.

PRESS FOLD Bring two creases together and press down the excess paper that is curved between them to create a new crease.

REVERSE FOLD The corner of an existing fold is creased, reversed, and folded over to the outside.

Folding Glossary

SQUASH FOLD	Start with at least two layers of paper. Make creases in the top layer. Lift the top layer, move it across, and then press down on the creases.	
TAP	Use your finger to tap where indicated to set off a preset series of folds.	
TRIM	The final adjustments to a paper plane so that it flies straight and true. This may involve adjustments to the ailerons, elevator, and rudder.	
VALLEY FOLD	Fold sides together so paper forms a V shape.	

Simple Flying Wing

This is one of the most basic of all paper airplanes. Composed solely of two wings, it has no tail, fuselage, or rudder. Be careful to make all the folds even, as too much deviation will result in an unstable flyer. Made correctly, the Simple Flying Wing is a good, stable glider. Examples of it can be seen in aviation, most prominently in the Northrop Flying Wing series.

1

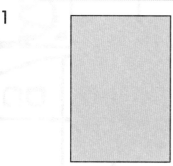

Begin with a sheet of A4 paper.

2

Fold the left side over to and even with the right side.

3

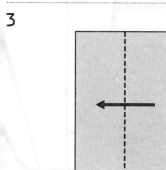

Unfold.

4

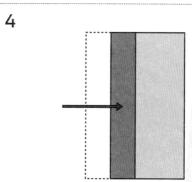

Fold the left side over to the center crease.

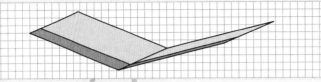

Simple Flying Wing

5

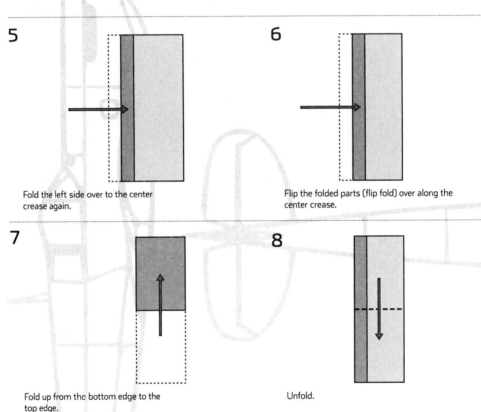

Fold the left side over to the center crease again.

6

Flip the folded parts (flip fold) over along the center crease.

7

Fold up from the bottom edge to the top edge.

8

Unfold.

In the air, the Simple Flying Wing should have a slight positive dihedral, as shown. To launch, grasp the plane from the back, lift it as high as you can, and release.

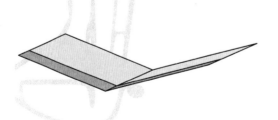

Standard

Here is a plane design that is truly international. I recently met a Russian woman who had made this in her childhood. It is exactly the same design I learned growing up in Iowa. Capable of fast speed and accuracy, the Standard will streak across the sky!

1

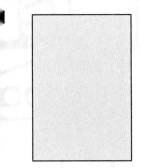

Begin with a sheet of A4 paper.

2

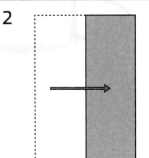

Fold the left side over to and even with the right side.

3

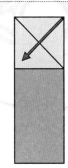

Fold the top right corner down to the left side.

4

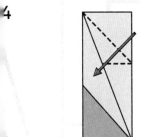

Fold the right side over to the left side as shown.

5

Fold again from the right side over to the left side as shown.

6

Flip over, from left to right.

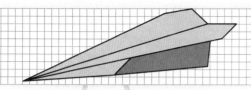

Standard

7

Fold the top left corner down to the right side.

8

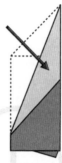

Fold from the left side over to the right side as shown.

9

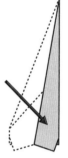

Fold the left side over to the right side again, as shown.

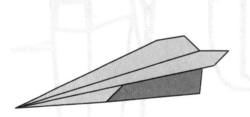

Unfold, and pop up the wings to give a slight positive dihedral, as shown. This plane will fly far and fast if you grasp it along the fuselage and throw it as hard as you can!

Traditional

Another well-known design, the Traditional reverses a lot of the folds of the Standard. It tucks the folds inside to make a more aerodynamic plane, and it also incorporates a couple of wingtip "rudders" to make it fly straight.

Begin with a sheet of A4 paper.

2

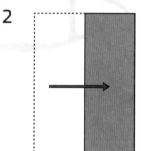

Fold the left side over to and even with the right side.

3

Unfold.

4

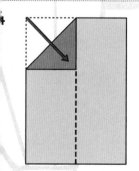

Fold the top left corner down.

5

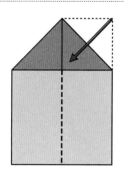

Repeat the same fold with the top right corner.

6

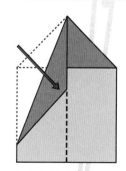

Fold the left side down to the center.

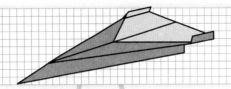

Traditional

7

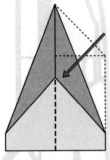

Repeat with the right side.

8

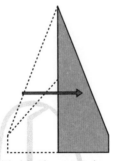

Fold the left side over to and even with the right side.

9

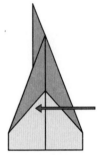

Take the top wing and fold it over to the le leaving about 1.2 inches (3 cm) of fuselag

10

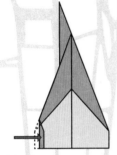

Fold the left wing tip up 0.4 inches (1 cm).

11

Flip over, from left to right.

12

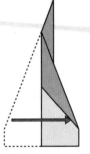

Fold the left wing over to the right, leavin about 1.2 inches (3 cm) of fuselage.

13

Fold the right wing tip over to the left 0.4 inches (1 cm).

Fold the wings up, and make the wing tips upright. This plane will fly just as hard and fast as you can throw it!

Improved Traditional

This is my improved version of the Traditional. It features a thicker airfoil for a smoother, stable flight. It will need a little up elevator, but with some practice you will be rewarded with a great flying plane!

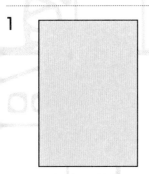

1

Begin with a sheet of A4 paper.

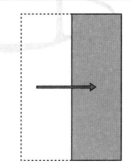

2

Fold the left side over to and even with the right side.

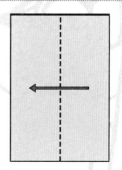

3

Unfold.

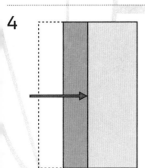

4

Fold the left side over to the center.

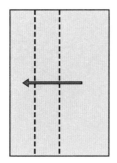

5

Unfold.

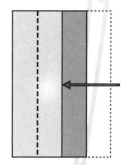

6

Fold the right side over to the center.

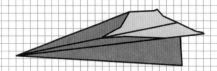

Improved Traditional

7

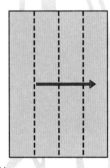

Unfold.

8

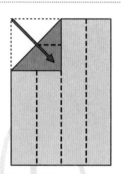

Fold the top left corner down to the center crease.

9

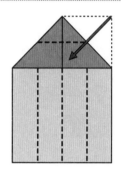

Repeat the same fold with the top right corner.

10

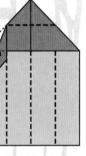

Take the left side and fold to the first crease.

11

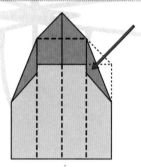

Repeat on the right side, folding to the first crease.

12

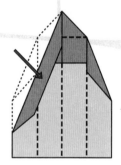

Take the left side over to the center crease as shown.

13

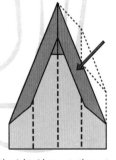

Take the right side over to the center crease as shown.

14

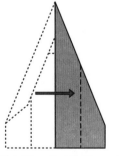

Fold in half from the left side over to and even with the right side.

15

Fold the top wing over from the right side to the left side, keeping it even with the left side.

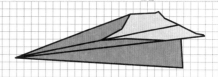

16

Flip over, from left to right.

17

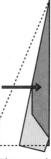

Fold the left side over to the right side, keeping it even with the right side.

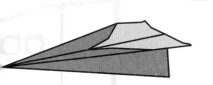

The Improved Traditional has a nice, smooth glide, and can be very accurate! This plane will take as fast a throw as you can muster!

Simple Dart

For a truly speedy flyer, try this little number. With minimal wing area, it has little drag. Of course, that also means that it requires a high airspeed to make it fly.

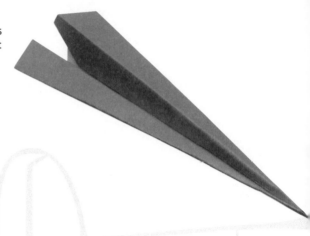

1

Begin with a sheet of A4 paper.

2

Fold the left side over to and even with the right side.

3

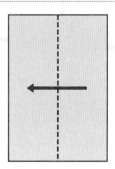

Unfold.

4

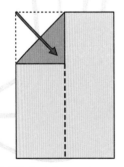

Fold the top left corner down.

5

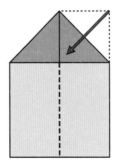

Repeat the same fold with the top right corner.

6

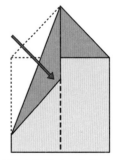

Fold the left side down to the center crease.

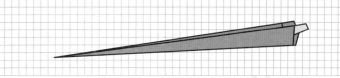

7

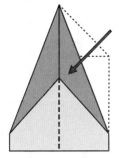

Repeat with the right side.

8

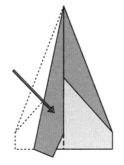

Fold the left side over to the center crease again.

9

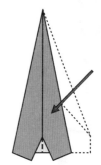

Fold the right side over to the center crease.

10

Fold the left side over to the center.

11

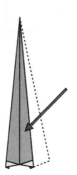

Fold the right side over to the center.

12

Flip over, from left to right.

13

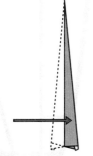

Fold the left side over to the right side.

This is a very sleek and speedy paper airplane. Throw with all your strength to make the Simple Dart fly fast and far!

Javelin

Much like the track and field spear this plane is named after, the Javelin is truly meant for distance competitions.

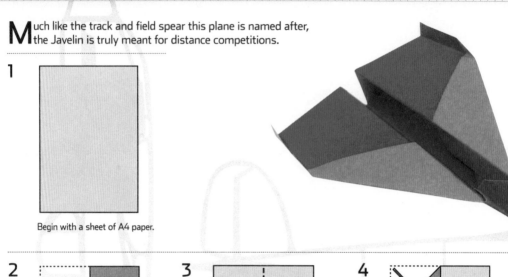

1

Begin with a sheet of A4 paper.

2

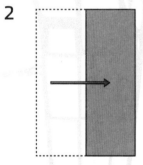

Fold the left side over to and even with the right side.

3

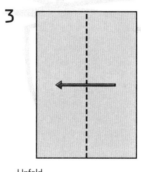

Unfold.

4

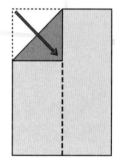

Fold the top left corner down.

5

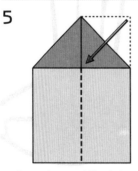

Repeat the same fold with the top right corner.

6

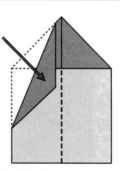

Fold the left side in, stopping 0.6 inches (1.5 cm) from the center crease.

7

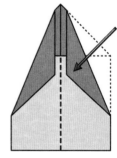

Repeat on the right side, stopping 0.6 inches (1.5 cm) from the center crease.

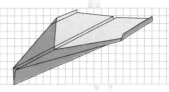

8

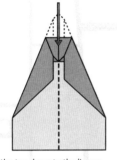

Fold the top down to the line as shown.

9

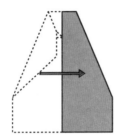

Fold the left side over to and even with the right side.

10

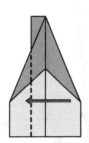

Fold the top wing to the left, starting at the top right corner and keeping the bottom edge even.

11

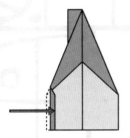

Fold the left side in 0.4 inches (1 cm).

12

Flip over, from left to right.

13

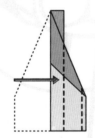

Fold the left side over to the right side, keeping the left edge even with the wing beneath it.

14

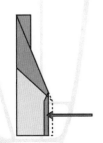

Fold the right side in 0.4 inches (1 cm).

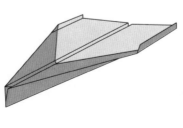

This is a great and graceful distance flyer. It may need a little up elevator, but in still air, the Javelin will fly straight and far!

Middleweight

Not all planes carry all of the weight in the nose. Sometimes you just have to mix things up a little and try something new!

1

Begin with a sheet of A4 paper.

2

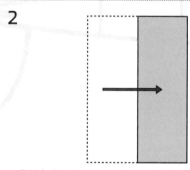

Fold the left side over to and even with the right side.

3

Unfold.

4

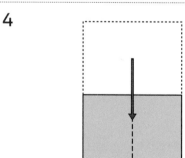

Fold the top edge down to and even with the bottom edge.

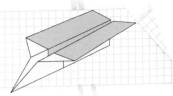

5

Unfold.

6

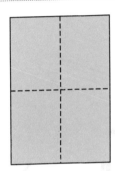

Flip over, from left to right.

7

Fold the top edge down to the center.

8

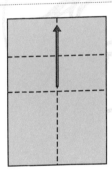

Unfold.

9

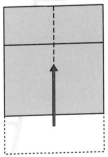

Squash fold the center horizontal crease up to the three-quarter crease.

10

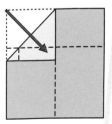

Fold the top left corner down to and even with the vertical center crease.

23

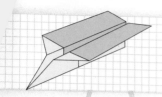

Middleweight

11

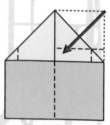

Fold the top right corner down to and even with the vertical center crease.

12

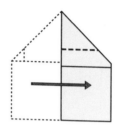

Fold the left side over to and even with the right side.

13

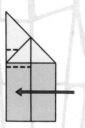

Fold the top right layer over to and even with the left side.

14

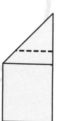

Flip over, from left to right.

15

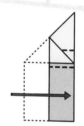

Fold the left side over to and even with the right side.

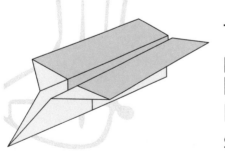

The Middleweight differs from most planes in that a large portion of its balancing weight is near the middle. It will only take a gentle toss to send it soaring across the room!

Doppelganger

At first glance, the Doppelganger looks a lot like the Middleweight. But it is a result of different folds, and it flies a little differently. That is why it is called the Doppelganger, which means "twin" or "look-alike."

1

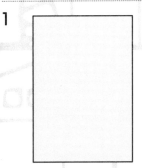

Begin with a sheet of A4 paper.

2

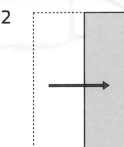

Fold the left side over to and even with the right side.

3

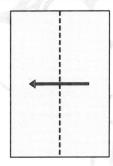

Unfold.

4

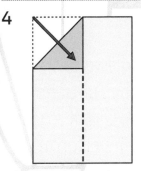

Fold the top left corner down to the center crease.

5

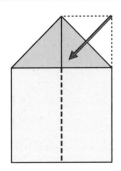

Repeat the fold with the top right corner.

6

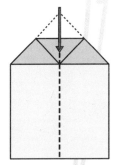

Fold the point down to the line.

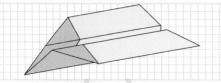

Doppelganger

7

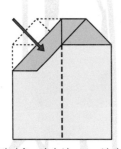

Fold the left angled side even with the center crease as shown.

8

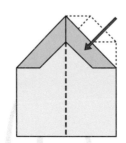

Repeat with the right angled side.

9

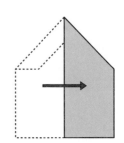

Fold the left side over to and even with the right side.

10

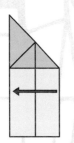

Fold the top wing over to and even with the left side.

11

Flip over, from left to right.

12

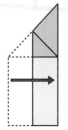

Fold the top wing over to and even with the right side.

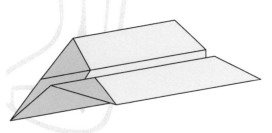

Unlike the Middleweight, the Doppelganger has all of its weight up front. Give it a gentle toss and watch it perform!

Cyrano

Cyrano de Bergerac was a Frenchman who was reputed to have a large nose that he was quite proud of. I think he would be proud of the plane I named after him, which has a large nose too!

1

Begin with a sheet of A4 paper.

2

Fold the left side over to and even with the right side.

3

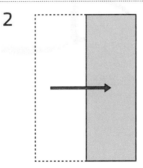

Unfold.

4

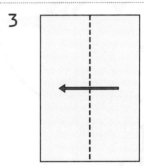

Fold the top edge down to the bottom edge.

5

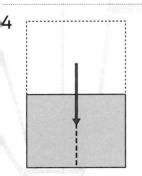

Unfold.

6

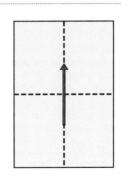

Fold the top down to the center crease.

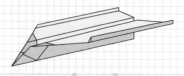

Cyrano

7

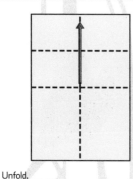

Unfold.

8

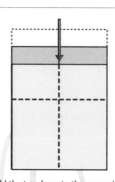

Fold the top down to the crease just created.

9

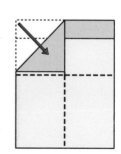

Fold the top left corner down to the center crease.

10

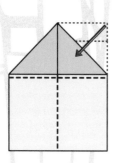

Fold the right corner down to the center crease.

11

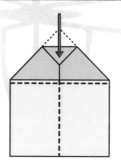

Fold the point down 1.4 inches (3.5 cm).

12

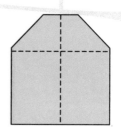

Flip over, from left to right.

13

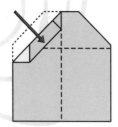

Fold the left angled side over to the center crease as shown.

14

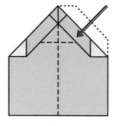

Fold the right angled side over to the center crease as shown.

15

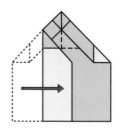

Fold the left side over to the right side 2.4 inches (6 cm).

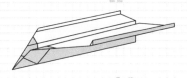

16

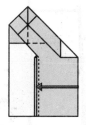

Fold the top wing over to the left
0.4 inches (1 cm).

17

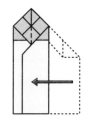

Fold the right side over to the left side
2.4 inches (6 cm).

18

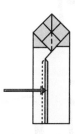

Fold the top wing over to the right
0.4 inches (1 cm).

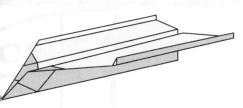

The Cyrano's large nose means it has lots of weight up front so you can throw it harder.

Afterburner

An afterburner is a component of some jet engines, placed after the main engine. Extra fuel is injected into the afterburner and burned for increased thrust. In this paper airplane, a spoiler is placed near the end to increase lift. Adding the spoiler to the stabilizers also makes it more stable!

1

Begin with a sheet of A4 paper.

2

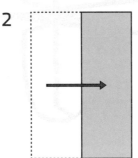

Fold the left side over to and even with the right side.

3

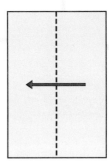

Unfold.

4

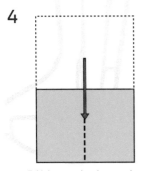

Fold the top edge down to the bottom edge.

5

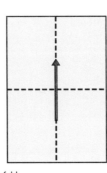

Unfold.

6

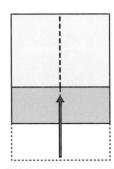

Fold the bottom edge up to the center crease.

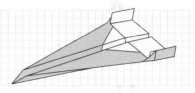

7

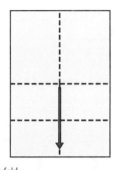

Unfold.

8

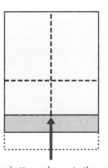

Fold the bottom edge up to the crease just created.

9

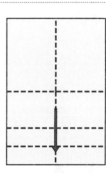

Unfold.

10

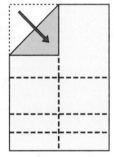

Fold the top left corner down to the vertical center crease.

11

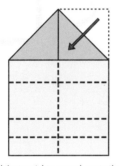

Fold the top right corner down to the vertical center crease.

12

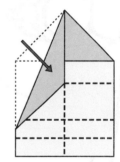

Fold the top left angled side over to the vertical center crease as shown.

13

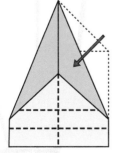

Fold the top right angled side over to the vertical center crease as shown.

14

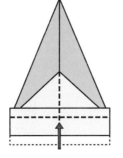

Now squash fold the lowest crease up to the one above it.

15

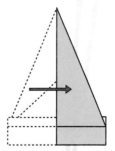

Fold the left side over to and even with the right side.

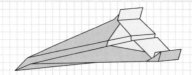

Afterburner

16

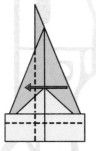

Fold the top wing over to the left, leaving 0.8 inches (2 cm) for the fuselage.

17

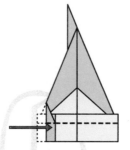

Fold the left side over 1 inch (2.5 cm).

18

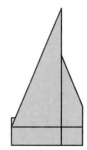

Flip, from left to right.

19

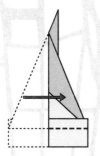

Fold the left side over so that the left side on top matches the fold below.

20

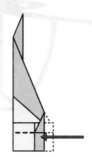

Fold the right side over 1 inch (2.5 cm).

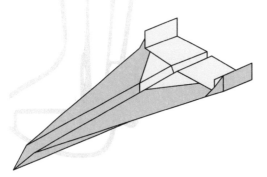

The Afterburner's additional reinforcement in the back provides it with extra lift and accuracy. Use it wisely!

Slow Jet

A slow jet sounds like an oxymoron, but it's a very apt name for this plane. Slow Jet looks sleek and fast, but it flies so slowly it seems almost stately.

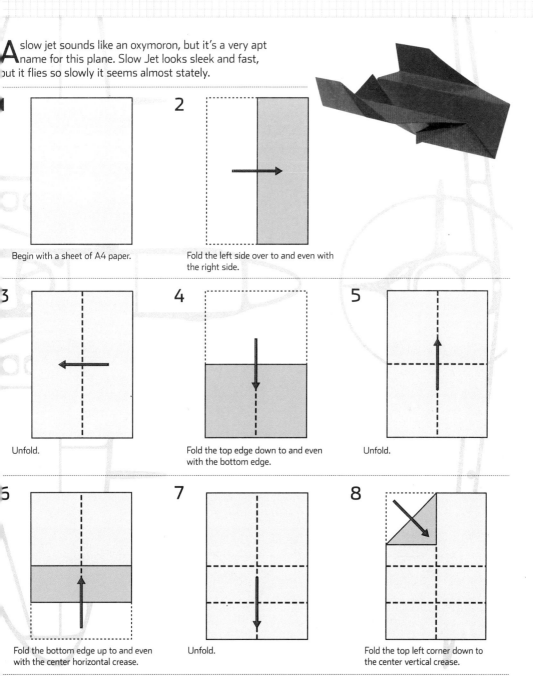

1

Begin with a sheet of A4 paper.

2

Fold the left side over to and even with the right side.

3

Unfold.

4

Fold the top edge down to and even with the bottom edge.

5

Unfold.

6

Fold the bottom edge up to and even with the center horizontal crease.

7

Unfold.

8

Fold the top left corner down to the center vertical crease.

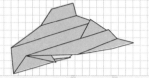

Slow Jet

9

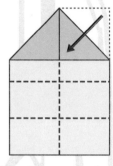

Fold the top right corner down to the center vertical crease.

10

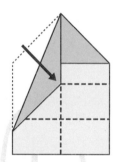

Fold the left angled side over to the center vertical crease.

11

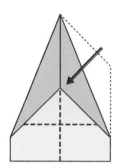

Fold the right angled side over to the center vertical crease.

12

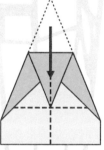

Fold the top point down to the intersection of the creases.

13

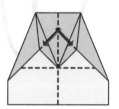

Unfold from below the point outwards as shown.

14

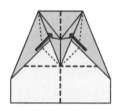

Fold the sides back onto the point as shown.

15

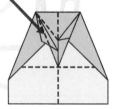

Squash fold the left side as shown.

16

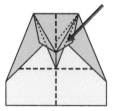

Squash fold the right side as shown.

17

Flip over, from left to right.

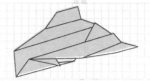

18

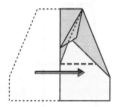

Fold the left side over to the right side.

19

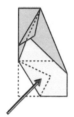

Push fold inside the bottom left corner, creating a tail fin.

20

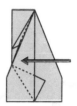

Fold the top layer from the right side over to the left side, using the upper right corner as a pivot.

21

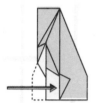

Fold the left side over to the right side, using the last fold as the end point.

22

Flip over, from left to right.

23

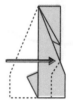

Fold the left side over to the right side, using the upper left corner as a pivot.

24

Fold the right side over to the left side, using the last fold as the end point.

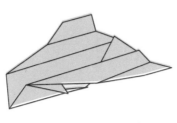

Pop open the wings and square out the lower squash folds. This plane will glide slow and true.

Thick-Winged Delta

A delta wing is a type of wing that is shaped like a triangle. This plane has deltas, with a thick airfoil to keep it in flight!

1

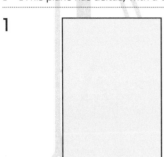

Begin with a sheet of A4 paper.

2

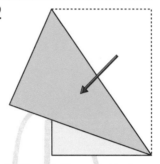

Fold the right side over, creasing from corner to corner.

3

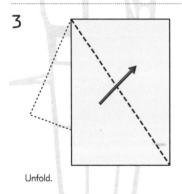

Unfold.

4

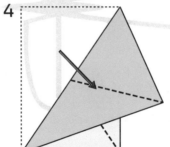

Repeat the fold from the left side over, and crease from corner to corner.

5

Unfold.

6

Flip over, from left to right.

7

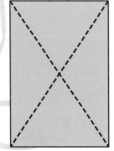

Fold the top edge down to the bottom.

8

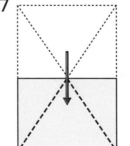

Unfold.

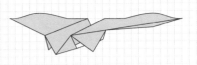

9

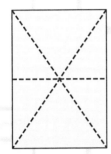

Flip over, from left to right.

10

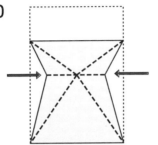

Tap the center of the "X" and then push in from the sides, folding in one side completely, then the other side as shown.

11

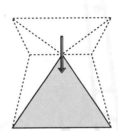

Press firmly down on the top to make a triangle.

12

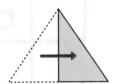

Fold the left side over to and even with the right side.

13

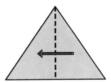

Unfold.

14

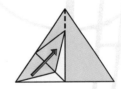

Fold the top layer on the left side up to the center crease.

15

Fold the top layer on the right side up to the center crease.

16

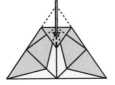

Fold the top point down so that the crease is even with the last two folds.

17

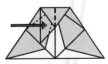

Fold the top layer on the left side over to the center crease.

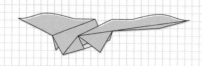

Thick-Winged Delta

18

Fold the top layer on the right side over to the center crease.

19

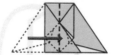

Fold the left side over to the right side as shown.

20

Unfold.

21

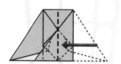

Fold the right side over to the left side as shown.

22

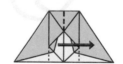

Unfold.

23

Flip over, from left to right.

24

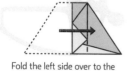

Fold the left side over to the right side.

Insert a finger into the delta wings and make them puffy. You may need to put a little up elevator on this plane. It's a nice slow flyer.

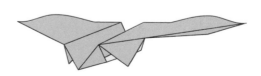

Nakamura Lock

I only wish I had come up with this classic design myself. I am still trying to find out who did so originally, as it appears in many books about paper planes. The Nakamura Lock is a truly graceful flyer, and worth including in any book on paper planes!

1

Begin with a sheet of A4 paper.

2

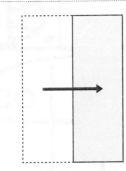

Fold the left side over to and even with the right side.

3

Unfold.

4

Fold the top left corner down to the center crease as shown.

5

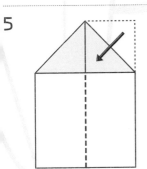

Fold the top right corner down to the center crease as shown.

6

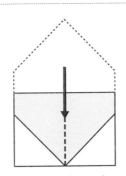

Fold the top point down to the bottom edge.

7

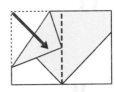

Fold the top left corner down to the center of the vertical crease.

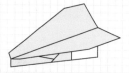

Nakamura Lock

8

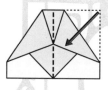

Fold the top right corner down to the center of the vertical crease.

9

Fold the point up to lock in the sides as shown.

10

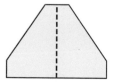

Flip over, from left to right.

11

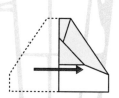

Fold the left side over to and even with the right side.

12

Fold the top right edge over to and even with the left edge as shown.

13

Flip over, from left to right.

14

Fold the top left edge over to and even with the right edge as shown.

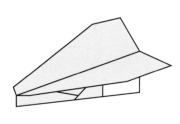

Pop the wings up, and grip the fuselage near the middle. Give the plane a good throw and watch it soar!

RTM

RTM (Return To Me) is such a cool-looking plane.
Be careful when you fly it, though!

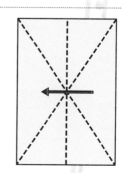

1

Begin with a sheet of A4 paper.

2

Fold the right side over, making a crease from the top left corner to the bottom right corner.

3

Unfold.

4

Fold the left side over, making a crease from the top right corner to the bottom left corner.

5

Unfold.

6

Flip over, from left to right.

7

Fold the left side over to the right side.

8

Unfold.

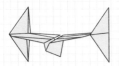

9

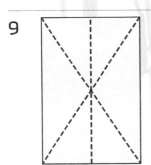

Flip over, from left to right.

10

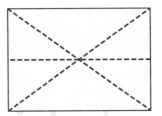

Rotate the paper 90 degrees, so that the long sides are at the top and the bottom.

11

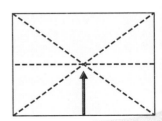

Press in at the center.

12

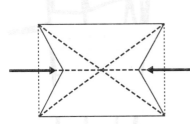

Fold the sides in and the top down.

13

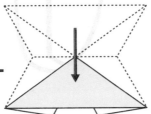

Press firmly down on the top to get the result shown.

14

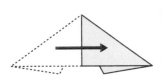

Fold the left side over to and even with the right side.

15

Unfold.

16

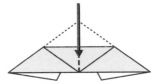

Fold the top point down to and even with the bottom as shown.

17

Fold the top layer on the left over 1.6 inches (4 cm), following the angle of the paper as shown.

18

Repeat on the top layer on the right side.

19

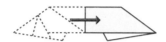

Fold in half again.

20

Fold the top layer on the right over 1.6 inches (4 cm), matching the layer below.

21

Fold the top wing over to the left, matching the angle shown.

22

Flip over, from left to right.

23

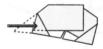

Fold the left side over 1.6 inches (4 cm), matching the layer below.

24

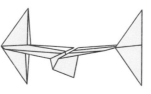

Fold the left wing over, matching the wings below.

The RTM is a trick flyer. Unfold the wings so they are level, and unfold the winglets so they are straight up and straight down. Tossed at a gentle angle into the sky, it will stall, flip over, and return to you!

Gullwing

This plane has wings shaped in the style of a gull. Gull wings have been the inspiration for many airplane designs throughout the years, and some car doors look like them too!

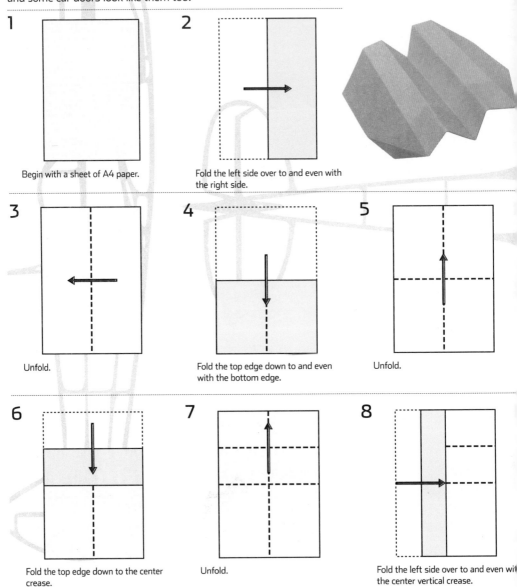

1

Begin with a sheet of A4 paper.

2

Fold the left side over to and even with the right side.

3

Unfold.

4

Fold the top edge down to and even with the bottom edge.

5

Unfold.

6

Fold the top edge down to the center crease.

7

Unfold.

8

Fold the left side over to and even with the center vertical crease.

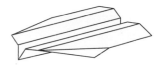

Gullwing

9

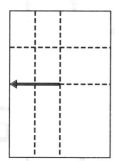

Unfold.

10

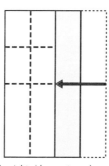

Fold the right side over to and even with the center vertical crease.

11

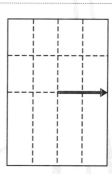

Unfold.

12

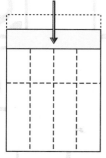

Fold the top edge down to and even with the first horizontal crease.

13

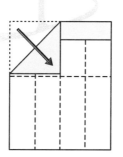

Fold the top left corner down to and even with the center vertical crease.

14

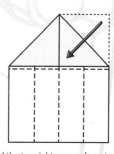

Fold the top right corner down to and even with the center vertical crease.

15

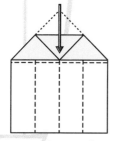

Fold the top point down to and even with the two previous folds.

16

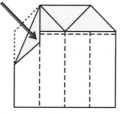

Fold the left angled side alongside the first vertical crease.

17

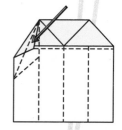

Squash fold the edge as shown.

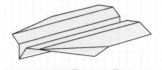

Gullwing

18

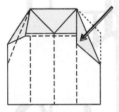

Fold the right angled side alongside the first vertical crease.

19

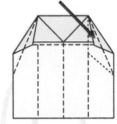

Squash fold the edge as shown.

20

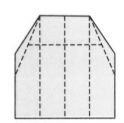

Flip over, from left to right.

21

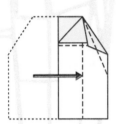

Fold the left side over to and even with the right side.

22

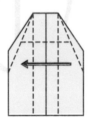

Fold the top layer over to the left, halfway across the top edge.

23

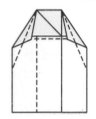

Flip over, from left to right.

24

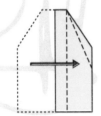

Fold the left side over to and even with the right side.

Pop open the wings as shown, and make sure they are angled alike. A very sensitive flyer, the Gullwing only requires a slow throw to send it cruising!

Vector

Named Vector for the capital "V" it resembles, this plane has an otherworldly appearance. It is an unusual aircraft in that it has twin wings on each side.

1

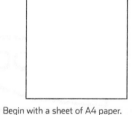

Begin with a sheet of A4 paper.

2

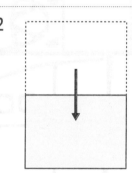

Fold the top edge down to the bottom edge.

3

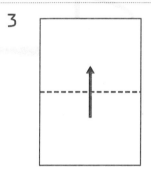

Unfold.

4

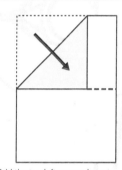

Fold the top left corner down to the center crease.

5

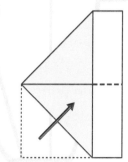

Fold the bottom left corner up to the center crease.

6

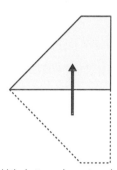

Fold the bottom edge up to and even with the top edge.

7

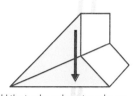

Fold the top layer down to and even with the bottom edge as shown.

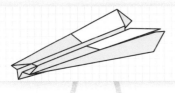

Vector

8	9	10

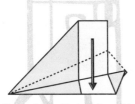

Continue by folding the top edge of this layer to the bottom edge as shown.

Flip over, from left to right.

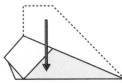

Fold the top layer down to and even with the bottom edge as shown.

11	12	13

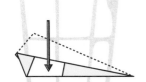

Continue by folding the top edge of this layer to the bottom edge as shown.

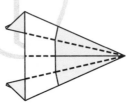

Open up, so that the view shown is the view from above.

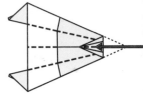

Fold the right point to the left 2 inches (5 cm).

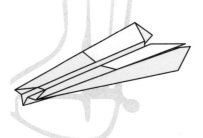

Now open up the wings, expand them a little, and give Vector a nice straight toss. If it dives, then open the wings up further, or give it a little up elevator.

Interceptor

Small and swift, the Interceptor accelerates to a good height with a strong throw. Be careful to make sure that the angles are sharp and even!

Begin with a sheet of A4 paper.

2

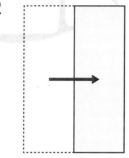

Fold the left side over to and even with the right side.

3

Unfold.

4

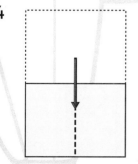

Fold the top edge down to and even with the bottom edge.

5

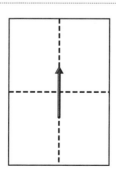

Unfold.

6

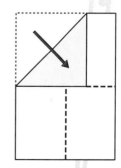

Fold the top left corner down to the center horizontal crease.

49

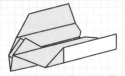

Interceptor

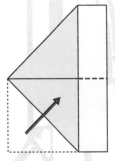

7

Fold the bottom left corner up to the center horizontal crease.

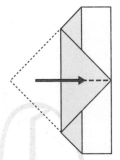

8

Fold the left point over to the right side.

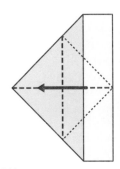

9

Unfold.

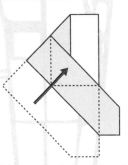

10

Fold the left point up to the crease located along the angled side and crease. Be sure to keep it even along the angled edge.

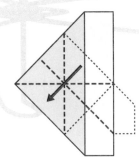

11

Unfold.

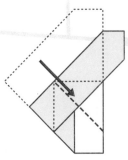

12

Fold the left point down to the crease located along the angled side. Be sure keep it even along the angled edge.

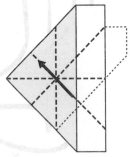

13

Unfold.

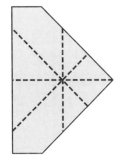

14

Flip over, from left to right.

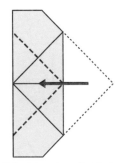

15

Fold the right point to the left side.

16

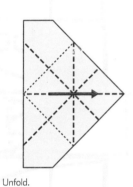

Unfold.

17

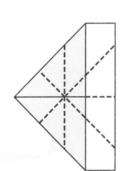

Flip over, from left to right.

18

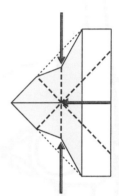

Press down in the center, and push in on the sides as shown.

19

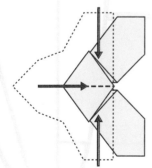

Continue pushing in on the sides, and press down on the top.

20

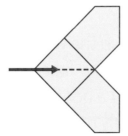

Continue pressing down on the top until the shape shown above appears.

21

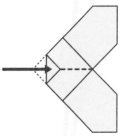

Fold the left point over to the right 1 inch (2.5 cm).

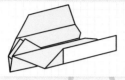

Interceptor

22

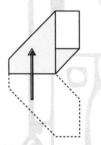

Fold the bottom edge up to and even with the top edge.

23

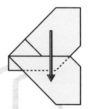

Fold the top layer down as far as possible on the left side, making sure the wing is horizontal.

24

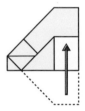

Fold the bottom edge up until it matches the bottom edge of the layer below.

25

Flip over, from left to right.

27

Fold the top down as far as possible on the right side, making sure the wing is horizontal.

27

Fold the bottom edge up until it matches the bottom edge of the layer below.

Pop up the wings and extend the winglets vertically. Take the Interceptor by the nose, give it a good strong throw, and watch it quickly gain altitude!

Baby Duck

This plane's little wings and little beak remind me of a baby duck! It won't have feathers, but it will fly on its baby wings.

1

Begin with a sheet of A4 paper cut down to a square 8 inches × 8 inches (210 mm × 210 mm).

2

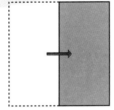

Fold the left side over to and even with the right side.

3

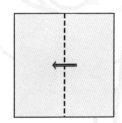

Unfold.

4

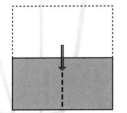

Fold the top edge down to and even with the bottom edge.

5

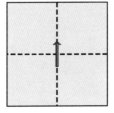

Unfold.

6

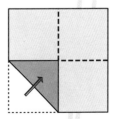

Fold the bottom left corner up to and even with the horizontal crease.

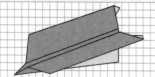

Baby Duck

7

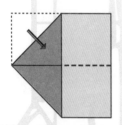

Fold the top left corner down to and even with the horizontal crease.

8

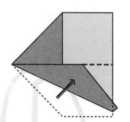

Fold the bottom left angled edge up to the horizontal crease.

9

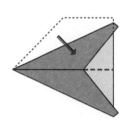

Fold the top left angled edge down to the horizontal crease.

10

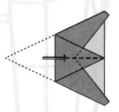

Fold the left point over to the right edge.

11

Unfold from below the triangle as shown.

12

Fold the top layer down to the horizontal crease as shown.

13

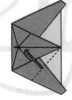

Fold the lower layer up to the horizontal crease as shown.

14

Fold the right point over to the left as far as it will go.

15

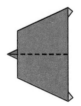

Flip over, from top to bottom.

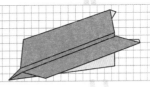

Baby Duck

16

Fold the bottom edge up to and even with the top edge.

17

Following the angle of the nose, fold the top layer down.

18

Flip over, from right to left.

19

Following the angle of the nose, fold the top edge down.

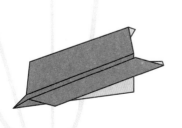

Pop the Baby Duck's wings up in a positive dihedral, and trim the plane using the triangle tabs at the end of the wings.

Hammerhead

A lot like the shark, this Hammerhead gains altitude and lift from the canard wing in the front. Not often seen these days, a canard is usually a small wing near the nose of a plane. Canards have certain advantages and disadvantages. Use this plane to discover what they are!

1

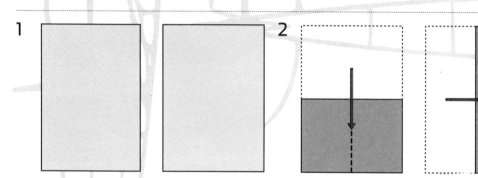

Begin with two sheets of A4 paper.

2

Fold the first sheet from the top edge to the bottom edge. Fold the second sheet from the left side over to the right side.

3

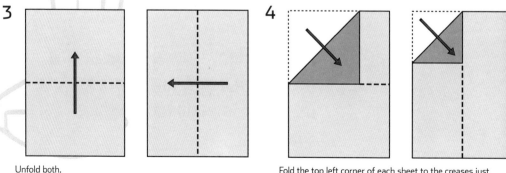

Unfold both.

4

Fold the top left corner of each sheet to the creases just created.

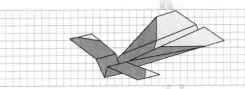

5

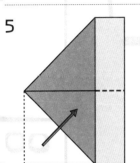 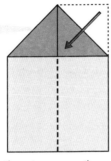

Fold the bottom left corner up to the center crease on the first sheet. Fold the top right corner down to the center crease on the second sheet.

6

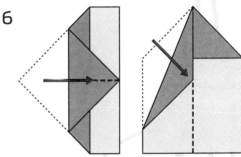

Fold the left point over to the right edge on the first sheet. Fold the left angled side to the center crease on the second sheet.

7

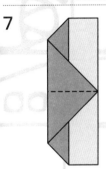 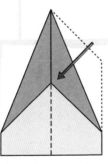

Fold the right angled side to the center crease on the second sheet.

8

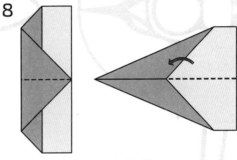

Turn the second sheet to the left 90 degrees.

9

 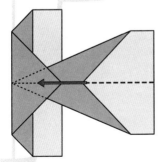
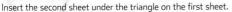

Insert the second sheet under the triangle on the first sheet.

10

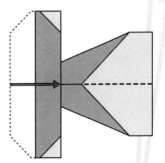

Fold the left side over to and even with the right side of the first sheet.

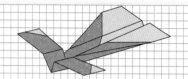

Hammerhead

11

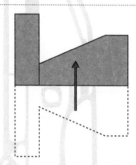

Fold the bottom edge up to and even with the top edge.

12

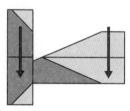

Fold the top layer down on both sheets, keeping the second sheet even with the bottom edge, and the first sheet even with the top edge of the second sheet.

13

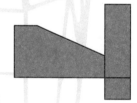

Flip over, from left to right.

14

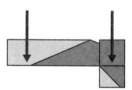

Fold the top edge of the left wing down to the bottom edge, and then fold the right wing down, keeping it even with the new top edge on the left wing.

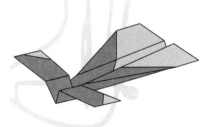

Adjust the four wings so they stick out from the plane at a 90-degree angle, then send your Hammerhead off in search of the sky!

Jart

A long time ago, I used to have a toy called Jarts. It was essentially a large Jart, which at nearly 19 inches (48 cm) is exactly the length of this plane!

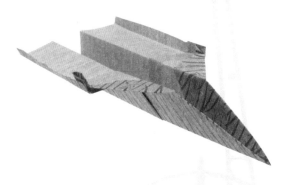

1

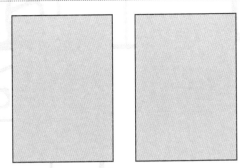

Begin with two sheets of A4 paper.

2

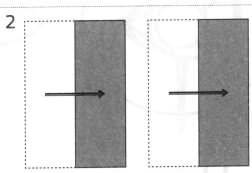

Fold both sheets from the left side over to the right side and firmly crease.

3

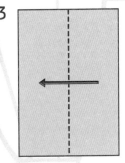
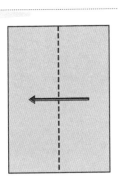

Unfold both.

4

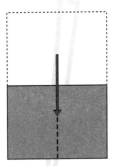

Fold the top edges of both sheets down to and even with the bottom edges and firmly crease.

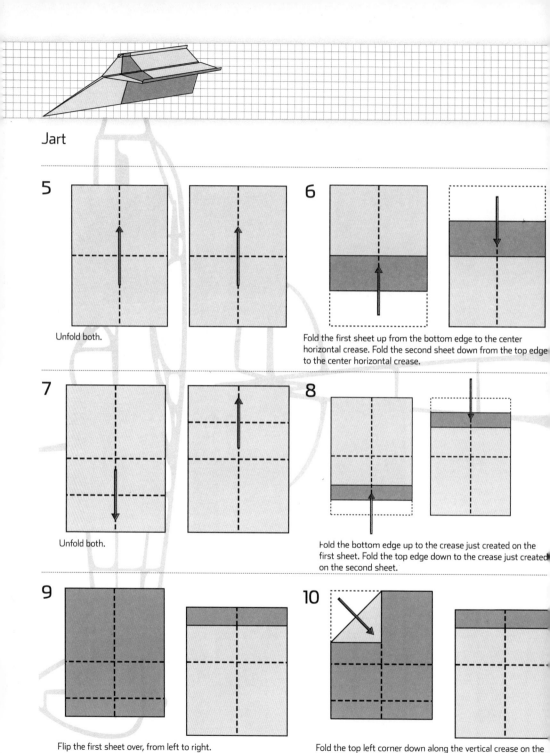

Jart

5

Unfold both.

6

Fold the first sheet up from the bottom edge to the center horizontal crease. Fold the second sheet down from the top edge to the center horizontal crease.

7

Unfold both.

8

Fold the bottom edge up to the crease just created on the first sheet. Fold the top edge down to the crease just created on the second sheet.

9

Flip the first sheet over, from left to right.

10

Fold the top left corner down along the vertical crease on the first sheet.

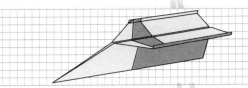

11

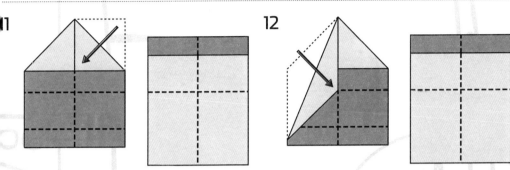

Fold the top right corner down along the vertical crease on the first sheet.

12

Fold the top angled side on the left down to the vertical crease on the first sheet.

13

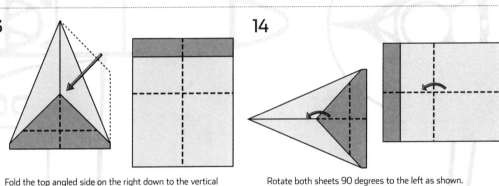

Fold the top angled side on the right down to the vertical crease on the first sheet.

14

Rotate both sheets 90 degrees to the left as shown.

15

Slide both sheets' folded edges together as shown.

16

Continue joining the sheets until the result shown above appears.

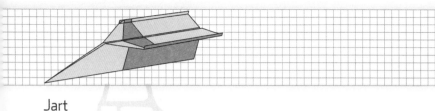

Jart

17

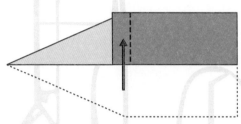

Fold the bottom edge up to and even with the top edge.

18

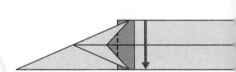

Fold the top layer down to and even with the bottom edge.

19

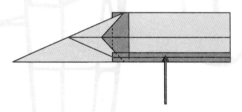

Fold the bottom edge up 0.4 inches (1 cm).

20

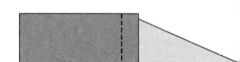

Flip over, from left to right.

21

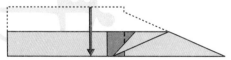

Fold the top edge down to and even with the bottom edge.

22

Fold the bottom edge up 0.4 inches (1 cm).

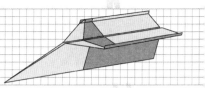

Jart

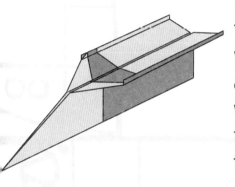

Not much is needed to make the Jart fly. Just ensure that the wings are even and the winglets are straight up. Be extra careful when you throw it, though, as this craft has a sharp point and is twice the weight of regular paper airplanes.

Index